GH00949865

Navigating

CASSELL&CO

First published in the United Kingdom in 2000 by Hachette UK
ISBN 1 84202 059 5

Designed by Chouka / Typeset in Sabon MT / Printed and bound in Germany

English translation by Prose Unlimited

Concept and editorial direction: Gheorghii Vladimirovitch Grigorieff

Additional editorial assistance: Colette Holden, Andrew Bolton, Jeremy Smith

A CIP catalogue for this book is available from the British Library.

Trademarks/Registered Trademarks

Hachette UK

Cassell & Co

The Orion Publishing Group

Wellington House

125 Strand

London

WC2R 0BB

Contents

What you will find in this book

1. An introduction to help you understand the Internet and the World Wide Web, and what a site is.

2. How to use Internet Explorer, a browser that will help you find your way round Internet sites.

3. The various features of other Internet browsers.

4. The addresses of dozens of sites you can start visiting.

5. Prompts to help you remember Internet Explorer shortcuts on the keyboard and a glossary.

Using what you'll learn from this book to back you up, you'll be able to join countless other Net surfers on the Information Super Highway.

1

Introduction

Introduction

The Internet is a gigantic network made up of millions of computers located all over the world. When you contact the Internet, your computer joins this network and you immediately gain access to the numerous services available: electronic mail, games, 'chat rooms', searching for and accessing all kinds of information, e-commerce, shopping, downloading documents and software programs.

This book will help you to navigate, or 'surf', your way around the millions of sites available throughout the world from Paris to Patagonia and from Honolulu to Hamburg.

You really don't need to be a computer expert to surf the Net. All you need is a computer, a modem and an access provider and you'll be ready to hop on and off the Information Super Highway at will.

As with many other things, the world of the Internet has its own jargon which is not always easy to understand at first, so if you think a 'cookie' is just something you dunk in your mid-morning coffee, take a look at the glossary at the end of this book. As you progress you will find that the jargon that seemed incomprehensible at first is actually a lot of fun. In fact the Internet itself is a lot of fun, so get online and start navigating your way around the virtual world .....

What exactly is the Internet?

So, you know that the Internet, or the 'Net', is a vast network linking up millions of computers all over the world, but, to be a little more precise, the Internet is made up of countless networks of interconnected computers. This is why the Internet is also sometimes called 'the Network of Networks'. These networked computers are permanently connected to the Internet by telephone lines, cables and satellite links. Being connected to the Internet is known as being 'online'.

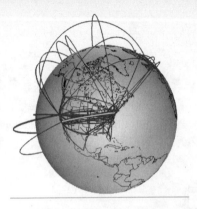

Source: An Atlas of Cyberspace
http://www.mappingcyberspace.com

When individual users connect up to the Internet, they do so via an Internet Access Provider (IAP), also known as a Service Provider (ISP). An Access Provider sells connections to the Internet. The computers of Access Providers are connected up permanently to the Internet, forming a bridge between the computers of the

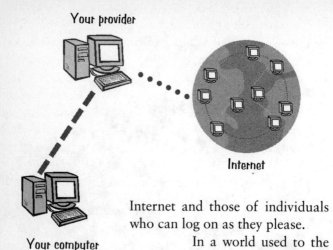

Your provider

Internet

Your computer

Internet and those of individuals who can log on as they please.

In a world used to the concept of ownership, whether private, corporate or state ownership, the odd thing about the Internet is that nobody owns it. There is no company, organisation, or even country owning or controlling the Internet. In any case, how could something so vast, which you can't even see, be controlled or policed by any one body? You could therefore say that the Internet belongs to everyone and certainly to all of its users. As a result, a series of unwritten rules of good conduct on the Net are developing spontaneously which are collectively known as Netiquette (Net-etiquette). These apply particularly to services where users interact directly with each other, such as e-mail and news groups.

The World Wide Web

Of all the services available on the Internet, the World Wide Web and electronic mail, or e-mail, are the most popular. The Web, or just WWW as it's sometimes known, symbolises, as its name implies, the network of cables linking one computer to another. These computers are in turn home to Web sites created by companies, organisations, or individuals. Web sites contain a huge diversity of information about literally every subject under the sun, which is presented in the form of Web pages.

As you might guess, a Web site may consist of several Web pages. These may be composed of any combination of text, still or animated images, and sound and video clips. You can visit literally any site in the world if you know its address. There are millions of them and their number is growing daily. By the dawn of the new millennium, there were more than five million sites throughout the world, whilst in 1997 there were only one million. This means that the Web has grown by 400% in just a few years. To give you a further idea of its size, of the 201,000,000 surfers currently connecting up at least once a week, some 8.1 million are British and some 3 million are French, the current total for Europe coming to 36 million, whilst in the USA there are around 110 million. However, these figures are increasing every day, so by the time you read this they will doubtless already be out of date.

We are truly in the middle of the so-called dot.com revolution, probably the most significant world-wide development since the industrial revolution and certain to change our way of life in ways we can yet barely imagine.

What sort of things can you do on the World Wide Web?

You can check the weather situation in Sydney, book a flight to Las Vegas, print out a vegetarian recipe, buy Paul Simon's latest CD, visit the Louvre, find Pizzeria Luigi's phone number in Rome, look up information in the Encyclopaedia Britannica, learn about astronomy, find a job, find the German word for 'gazebo', obtain the football championship results, pursue a course in accounting, get information on the latest scientific developments, see what's happening in Miami or Paris at the very moment events are taking place..... The possibilities are endless.

How much does the Internet cost?

There are two types of charges to bear in mind, as well as the cost of the computer and the modem. First of all, you have to subscribe to an access or service provider. It is the provider that will give you access to the Internet and all its services. Many providers offer a subscription free of charge. With others, the subscriber pays a monthly fee, in return for, for example, free technical support. You will need to do some research and compare the pros and cons of the services which each of the access providers can offer.

Secondly, you have to pay the telephone costs; in accordance with the rates charged by your telecommunications operator. Typically these are just the cost of a local call, though if you are online for any length of time, the costs can soon mount up. However, some companies are now offering free access and free phone calls, so it pays to shop around and do some thorough research before you sign up with a provider.

Navigation software programs, also called 'browsers', are completely free of charge. Using the Internet itself is also completely free. The costs of maintaining the network are borne by organisations such as universities, companies and the countries that own the cables, computers and all the necessary equipment. At the end of the day however, users or not, we are all paying for the Internet in some way; whether it be through taxes or the effects of the Internet on the prices of the products we buy. Once logged onto the Net however, there are a few sites which require payment for their services, but otherwise you won't be asked to part with any money online – unless you wish to shop on the Net. If you are intending to buy something, you will have to provide a method of payment, such as a credit card number.

The computer equipment you need

The good news is that you don't need any particularly sophisticated equipment to get around on the Internet.

The hardware

All you really need is a standard computer for home use, which can be either a PC or a Macintosh. Its power, RAM and size of hard disk are not that important. A good screen and a 16 million colour graphic card will give you the best visual displays and enable you to appreciate better the quality of the sites you visit.

The speed with which you navigate depends mainly on the modem. You will need a model capable of transmitting at a speed of at least 33,600 bps (bits per second). A very fast modem (56,000 bps) will be more expensive, but is more convenient because of its greater speed.

The software

If you have a PC, it's most likely to be equipped with Microsoft's Windows Operating System. All versions of Windows can be used on the Internet. If you use a Macintosh, you can use all models and all Operating Systems for surfing the Net.

Microsoft's Internet browser, Internet Explorer 5, is used in this book, as the basis for explaining how to navigate your way around the Web. Explorer version 5 is provided free of charge with the second edition of Windows 98. But if you use another version or a different browser (Netscape Navigator, for example), you won't have any problem getting used to it as the procedures and method of navigation are almost the same, whatever browser you use. The Bookmarks feature peculiar to Netscape Navigator is explained in chapter five.

What browser do you use?

It's likely that a browser has already been installed in your system. Look under Office (Windows or Macintosh). You will see one of these two icons:

    Internet Explorer

    Netscape Navigator.

To find out what version of browser you have:

1 Double-click on its icon.

2 Choose the [?] command – About..., or [Help] – About...

3 Close the window by clicking on the OK button.

If there is no browser available on your computer, install it yourself or ask your access provider for help. You will often find the latest version of Internet Explorer or Netscape Navigator on CD-ROMs that are supplied with the many magazines devoted to the Internet, or the connection kit you receive from access providers. The installation procedure is very simple and more or less automatic.

2

Millions of sites to visit

Note

If you have an ISDN link, a high speed version of a normal phone line, you need a special modem called a Terminal Adapter, which is a little more expensive than the conventional ones, and an access provider that can provide ISDN access — again turn on the modem and activate the software from the access provider.

Millions of sites to visit

Surfing on the Web is very simple. All you have to do is connect up to the Internet, open your browser and type in the address of the site you want to visit. Here's how.

Getting connected

If you have a cable link, you simply turn on your computer and modem to be connected immediately to the Internet.

If you have an ADSL (asymmetrical digital subscriber line) connection, which is a high speed connection via telephone cable, turn on the modem and activate the special software you received from your access provider.

If you have an ordinary telephone line, use the following procedure:

 Turn on the modem.

 In Windows Desktop, double-click on the icon My Computer.

 Double-click on the folder Dial-up Networking.

 Double-click on the icon Internet Access.

 Type in your username and your password (this information appears on the documents given to you by your access provider). Then click on the Connect button.

It is possible that this dialogue box won't appear. This simply means that the information necessary for connecting up has already been entered previously.

The modem dials the phone number of your access provider's computer. A dialogue box displays the progress of the connection: numbering, password verification and finally the start of a session on the Net.

At the far right of the Windows toolbar, a small icon indicates that a connection is acti-ve. Your computer is now part of the Internet. You are online and are ready to start surfing. If you have just one telephone line, you will not be able to receive calls while you are surfing as the line is being monopolised by your Internet connection. Make sure you don't use the phone to make a call out, either, as that would interrupt your connection.

NB: Depending upon the terms of the subscription with your access provider, as soon as the Internet connection is established, you may be paying for the time you spend on the phone line, even if you are not actual-ly using the Internet.

To disconnect

 Click with the right mouse button on the little icon at the far right of the Windows 98 toolbar.

 Select the command Disconnect.

Opening your browser

If you want to visit Web sites, you will first have to open your navigating software, or browser

To open Internet Explorer

 Double-click on the Internet Explorer icon (usually located in Windows Desktop).

Internet Explorer

If the Internet Explorer icon is not in Desktop, you will find the command in the Start menu: click on the Start button, then on the Programs folder and finally on Internet Explorer.

 Closing your browser does not automatically disconnect you from the Internet. You must make sure that you disconnect using the procedure explained above.

The Internet Explorer window

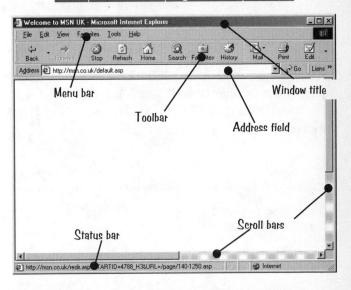

The main zones in the Internet Explorer window.

Once the connection has been established, the Internet Explorer window automatically opens at the MSN (Microsoft Network) site.

The commands

The menu bar contains all the available commands. To carry out a command, click on the menu and it will drop down. Then click on the name of the command you require.

The Refresh command
in the View menu.

The commands followed by
an arrow open a dialogue box.

Commands preceded by a tick
indicate that the option is active

To close the browser

Close the browser either by clicking
on the Close window, or by clicking
on File, then Close.

Web site addresses

How do you get access to a site? Imagine the World
Wide Web as an enormous city. Each house is a site at
which the owners puts what they want on show. This could
be anything from a collection of stamps and family photos, to a catalogue of products they are selling, and so on.
The various rooms in the house are the site's Web pages.

Almost all Web sites can be accessed freely, you just
need to know their addresses. The address of a site always
begins with http://, which stands for Hyper Text Transfer

Protocol. This protocol specifies the way in which the data is transmitted from the site to your computer and it tells the browser that you want to view a Web site. It is a language shared by both Web sites and browsers.

For example:

> **http://www.birmingham.ac.uk**

is the address of Birmingham University's site.

The address of a site is called a Uniform Resource Locator, or 'URL', for short.

Every address is unique and the URL designates one site and one site only. Wherever your geographical location happens to be, the URL will always direct you to the same site.

You will soon notice that many addresses start with www (as in World Wide Web). However, this is not always the case, for example: http://encarta.msn.com is the address for the encyclopaedia Encarta.

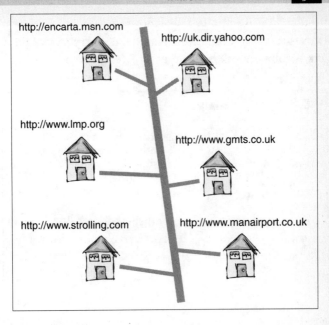

On the other hand, all addresses end with two or three letters that identify either the country where the site is to be found, or the type of site.

Examples of country suffixes			
uk	United Kingdom	**fr**	France
be	Belgium	**au**	Australia
ca	Canada	**dk**	Denmark
in	India	**za**	South Africa
dz	Algeria	**de**	Germany
il	Israel	**ma**	Morocco
ch	Switzerland	**se**	Sweden
nl	Holland	**jp**	Japan

Suffixes that are international			
com	Commercial	**edu**	Educational
gov	Government	**mil**	Military
net	Internet services provider		
org	Organisation (often non-profit-making)		

The information in a site is spread over several pages. When you type in the address of a site, the first thing you will see on screen is its welcome page. It's rather like the summary or contents list of a book.

However, you don't need to wade through the whole site in order to reach the page you want, if you happen to know it in advance. You can enter the name of the precise Web page you want to view as part of the site's address, for example:

http://encarta.msn.com/category/lifescience.asp

With this address you are asking to see the contents of the page entitled lifescience.asp in the site at the address http://encarta.msn.com. The pages of a site are stored on the hard disk of a computer, organised into a hierarchy of folders – just as in Internet Explorer. The page entitled lifescience.asp is located in the category folder on the hard disk containing the whole site.

Note

When you are typing in an address, make sure you enter the lower case and capital letters correctly. Web site addresses never contain letters with accents (e.g., , ,) or spaces, but they may contain numbers, dots, the underline character _ or a tilde ~ .

On an ordinary PC keyboard, the tilde is the third character of the [2] or [=] key. To display it, press the [AltGr] key and hold it down while you press either [2] or [=]. Then press the spacebar.

On the Macintosh Natural Keyboard, you press [Shift] and hold it down while you press the key preceding [1] (below Esc), then press a letter (e.g., to get) or the spacebar to get ~ on its own.

On a Macintosh, hold down the [Alt] key and type the letter n . Then press the spacebar.

Getting into a site

Click on the address box of your browser and type in the address of the site in which you are interested (for example: http://www.texascooking.com). Then press *Enter* or click or the *Go* button.

The little icon in the top right-hand corner of the window starts moving. This means that the browser is searching for the site and, if it finds

it, that it is displaying the data from the Web page. It keeps on moving until the whole of the Web page has been displayed.

So what's happening?

The data is being downloaded from the site you are visiting to your computer.

The browser program searches for the site whose address you have typed in. It sends the contents of the Web page you asked for to your computer. In other words, your browser downloads the data from the computer where the site is situated to your computer.

The Internet Explorer status bar shows you how the download is progressing, step by step.

For every site address comprised of words and letters, there is a numerical address, called the Internet Protocol, or IP address. The Internet organises the sites in a directory and locates them by memorising their numerical

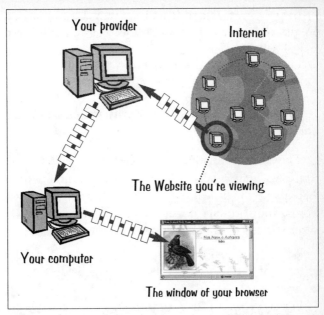

Your provider

Internet

The Website you're viewing

Your computer

The window of your browser

address. But, to make things easier for us ordinary human surfers, the Internet also keeps directories of Web sites in words and letters.

For example, the address http://www.marabout.com is equivalent to the IP address 196.46.198.75. It doesn't matter which of the two addresses you type into your browser, though it's much easier to remember www.marabout.com.

Specialised computers keep a list of concordances, like this:

www.marabout.com	196.46.198.75
www.yahoo.com	240.71.200.68
www.texascooking.com	205.238.148.22
www.altavista.com	204.152.190.13

When you press the *Enter* key, after having typed an address into your browser, the Web page is downloaded in three stages.

First stage

The address in words and letters is converted into a numerical address and the browser searches for the site.

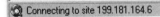

Second stage

The site is located. The browser waits for the first data that the site sends out to it.

Third stage

The Web page is downloaded from the computer hosting the site to your computer.

Opening page http://www.seanet.com/~tberry/Aa/recipe

The various elements of the page are downloaded a little at a time. The blue strip gets longer as the downloading nears completion.

The Home Page

When you enter a site, you are often welcomed to it with an introductory page, usually a summary page that will give you access to the other pages on the site. This is called the 'Home Page'. Generally speaking, this is the page which will automatically be downloaded to your computer if you do not specify a precise page in the address.

For example:

if you type the address

http://www. kidsplanet. org

you will receive the Home Page, but if you type

http://www. kidsplanet. org/wol/index. html

the index.html page in the site's wol directory will be displayed. To get to the Home Page, just delete everything that follows the site's address, keeping only http://www.kidsplanet.org.

Internet Explorer helps you to type in addresses

You don't always have to type in the full address of a site. There are a couple of handy features in Internet Explorer which make life just that little bit easier.

The address box of the browser behaves like a line in a word-processing document. You can move the cursor with the left and right arrows on your keyboard and insert characters at the point where the cursor is located, or delete characters using the Backspace and Delete keys.

The Clipboard function is active in all applications – as it is here too. If you copy an address from any type of document, you can paste it into the browser's address box, using the command *Edit/Paste* or using the keystrokes [Ctrl]-[c].

Abbreviating the address

Since all site addresses start with http://, you can ignore this part and type in the site's address directly. Internet Explorer will put in this header itself.

For example:

To view Yahoo's site (http://uk.yahoo.com), just type uk.yahoo.com and press *Enter*.

Second Feature

However, if a site's address starts with www and ends with .com, just type in the name and press [Ctrl–]-[Enter]. Internet Explorer completes the address automatically.

For example:

type texascooking, press *Ctrl* and hold it down while you press *Enter*.

The address list

When you type a few characters in the address box, a list will open. It offers sites whose address starts with the characters you have just typed in.

If the list is too long, type in a few more characters
to narrow the choice of sites offered.

Scroll through the contents of the list by using the cursor arrows and/or *Page Up* or *Page Down*.

Then click on the address you want, and you will access the site immediately – or use the ↓ or ↑ keys to select it and press *Enter* to confirm.

You can stretch the list out by dragging its bottom right-hand corner down.

You might wonder where these addresses have come from. Explorer has just been tidying up and doing a spot of housekeeping. It keeps a record of all the addresses of the sites you have already visited.

You don't have to type the header of the address or www to make the list function.

The Lyn Fone Bakery

Large Madeira Cake

For example

if you type ya, the list will show you sites whose address starts with http://www.ya.

Therefore, if you haven't yet visited any sites, this list will be blank.

If you have not already visited an address beginning with the characters you are typing in, the address box will remain blank, so you will have to type in the address in full.

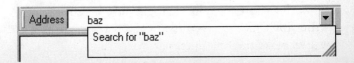

Semi-automatic keyboarding

Start typing in a complete address.

For example:

http://www.ya

Internet Explorer will open the address list, but may also take the initiative of finishing the address for you. Here too, Explorer takes the addresses of sites you have already visited as a basis.

This action is not activated when Internet Explorer is installed. But you can request it yourself.

Select the command *Tools/Internet Options* and click the *Advanced* tab in the dialogue box. Click on the little box in front of the option *Use inline AutoComplete for Web addresses*. Close the dialogue box by clicking the *OK* button.

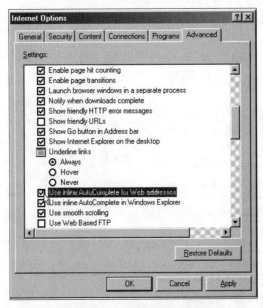

This option will make Internet Explorer
just that little bit more useful.

If there's a problem...

You've typed in the address of a site and, instead of displaying it, Internet Explorer shows you a page entitled 'The page cannot be displayed'. The Internet Explorer title bar gives you a further message: 'Cannot find server'.

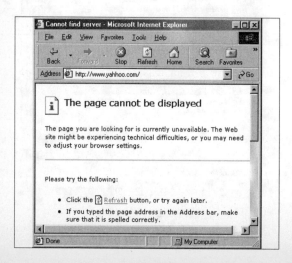

What's happening? Internet Explorer cannot find the site you want to visit. There are three main reasons for this kind of problem.

Are you connected to the Internet? Sudden disconnections are not uncommon. Check whether the little icon at the far right of the Windows toolbar is clearly visible.

You've made a typing error in the address. Check each character carefully.

The site no longer exists or has moved to another address.

Another problem you may encounter is that if you type in the address of a site, followed by the name of a precise Web page on that site, Internet Explorer may display another one of its pages, indicating 'The page cannot be found'. You may also find the header bar's window displaying the message: 'HTTP 404 not found'.

For example:

http://www. marabout. com/test. htm.

In this case, the site does exist, but the page you indicated does not. You may have made a typing error, but it is also possible that this page has been deleted from the site or renamed. The easiest thing to do then is to go back to the site's Home Page and delete any reference to a specific page in the address box, keeping only the principal address. In our example, delete /test.html. Then you're left with *http://www.marabout.com*. Press *Enter*.

Some error codes

Each type of error has a precise code. In the preceding example, the error code is 404. Here are a few of the most frequent error codes you are likely to encounter:

301	The site has been moved.
401	You are not authorised to visit this site.
403	The site has refused to allow you access to it.
404	The page has not been found on the site.
500	An error has occurred on the computer hosting the site.
503	The site exists, but does not respond because it is too busy or is temporarily out of service.

How do you find sites?

If you don't know what sites to visit in order to find the information you're looking for, you can use the free directory services or search engines.

The directories have lists of sites, categorised by subject. You can search for the sites in which you are interested by going through the categories and sub categories, or by using keywords.

On the other hand, search engines are rather like vast indexes of Web pages. They catalogue every page of each site, as distinct from the directories that catalogue sites without going into the details of their individual pages. You should therefore consult search engines for more precise investigations.

Here are the addresses of a few directories:

- Yahoo! US: http://www.yahoo.com

- Yahoo! UK: http://uk.yahoo.com

- Magellan: http://magellan.excite.com

- Infoseek: http://infoseek.go.com

Here are the addresses of a few search engines:

- Google: http://www.google.com

- Alta Vista: http://www.altavista.com

- whatUseek: http://whatuseek.com

3

Surfing

Surfing

You can surf from one Web page to another on the same site, or from one Web page to one on another site by clicking on hypertext links. These enable you to access other pages either on the same site, or located on other sites, very quickly.

Don't forget that all the techniques explained here for the World Wide Web also apply for consulting multimedia CD ROMs.

But, to start with, let's see how best to explore and view the page being displayed.

Exploring a Web page

The window

The dimensions of a Web page often exceed the size of the browser window, so you will need to use the scroll bars to view the whole page.

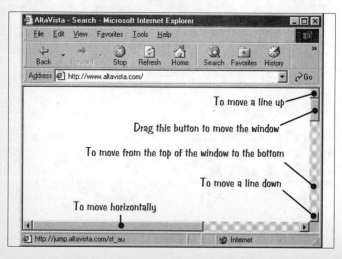

The browser window works like any other window, so you can move it, modify its size, or maximise it.

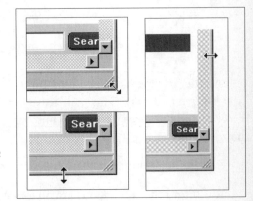

Changing the dimensions of a window.

Maximising the window and returning it to its original size.

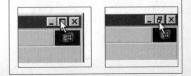

You can also use shortcut keys

To go to the top of the page	*Home*
To go to the end of the page	*End*
To scroll down the page	*Page Down* or
screen by screen	*Space bar*

Full screen display

In order to have as large a window as possible, opt for a full-screen display. This will leave you with just the toolbar and the three navigation buttons in the top right-hand corner.

Choose the command *View/Full Screen* or press *F11*.

You'll find that the menus are no longer available and the status bar is invisible, but the navigation buttons remain on display.

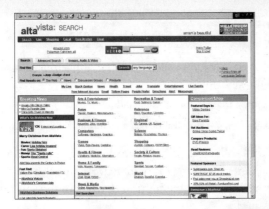

To return to a normal display, click on the window's *restore button* or press *F11*.

Searching for information

Web pages can be very long, making it difficult to find a particular item of information.

To find a piece of information within a page

 Press [Home] to position the cursor at the beginning of the page.

 Choose the command Edit/Find (on this page).

 Type in the text for which you are looking in the dialogue box. Click on the Find Next button.

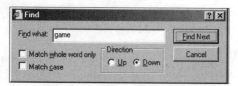

If you activate the option *Match whole word only*, the text for which you are looking will be considered as a whole word, so if you type in several words or groups of letters Explorer will look for this grouping as a whole.

By activating the option *Match case*, Explorer will search for whatever you enter in the dialogue box in exactly the same combination of lower case and upper case letters.

Note

This command searches only in the page displayed and not throughout the site, or throughout all the sites on the World Wide Web.

Hypertext links

A Web page is made up principally of text and images (still or animated) and, most importantly, hypertext links.

A hypertext link acts as a gateway, providing access to another page. By clicking on a hypertext link, you can jump directly from one page to another.

How will you recognise the presence of a hypertext link on a Web page? Drag the mouse over the page. As soon as the cursor changes into a little hand, the item to which it is pointing is a hypertext link.

It can take the form of either words or an image. The text representing a link is often underlined, though this is not always the case.

Click once on a hypertext link and the browser will download the page to which it is connected. Hypertext links are created by the Web site's designer. The page at the other end of a hypertext text link may be located somewhere else on the same site, but equally it may be on a site on the other side of the world. You just never know where you'll end up.

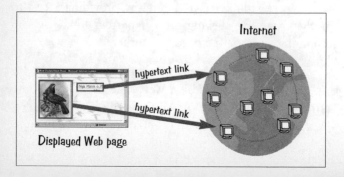

To find out the address of a link, position the cursor over it (without clicking) and the address will appear in the status bar.

 There is always a delay between the moment you click on a hypertext link and when the page is displayed.

This is quite normal, it is simply the time it takes for the page's data to reach your computer. You will find that when the Internet is very busy, you may have to wait a while for the page you want to appear.

If you can't wait, you can always interrupt the current download by clicking on the *Stop* button and pressing *Esc*. The items already downloaded will remain on display.

You will notice that the links often change colour once you have clicked on them. This simply shows that you have already viewed the page represented by this link. The colours are not standardised across the Internet however, as they are chosen by the site's designer. Nor is underlining links a general rule, again it depends upon the whims of the site's creator.

The windows

When you click on a hypertext link, the page to which it is connected opens either in the same window, or in a new window. It all depends on the way in which the link was programmed by the site's designer.

You can open new browser windows yourself. For example, click on a link with the right mouse button and choose the command *Open in new window*, the page to which the link is connected will be displayed in a new window.

If you want to open an additional window yourself, choose the command File/New/ Windows.

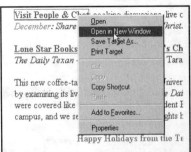

Each window opened is represented by a button in the Windows taskbar. You can move from one window to another by clicking on the buttons at the bottom of the screen.

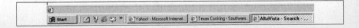

You can surf in each window independently. For example, while you are looking up recipes in one site, you can be searching in the Yahoo directory in another window and be visiting the personal site created by one of your friends in yet another.

Don't open too many windows however, otherwise Internet Explorer or Windows risks becoming saturated and freezing.

To close a window

Proceed as for any other window: click on the Close button in the top right-hand corner (the little 'x') or choose the command File/Close.

Leaving a trail

With the aid of hypertext links, you don't need to leaf page by page through a Web site as you do with a book, you can jump immediately to the page of your choice. The browser memorises each page you visit and logs the information, rather like in a travel diary where you record the places you have visited. You can scroll through this diary, using the *Back* and *Forward* buttons, to find the pages you have already visited. However, you cannot view the site page by page with these buttons.

Let's take an example:

Imagine you visited the following pages successively:

Which pages will you display by clicking on the *Back* and *Forward* buttons?

If you prefer, you can choose the exact page to which you wish to return. Instead of clicking on the button, click on the little arrow to its right and the list of pages visited will appear. Click on the one you want to view again.

Note

Internet Explorer stores in memory the succession of pages visited for each window independently and loses all trace of your visits as soon as you close the window.

Temporary files

Internet Explorer stores a copy of all the pages visited and the items they contain, such as images, on your hard disk. These temporary files are automatically stored in a special folder called *Internet Temporary Files*, *Cache memory* or *Pre-memory*. This data, unlike the pages available through the *Back* and *Forward* buttons, does not disappear when you close your browser. It is not stored in RAM, but saved on the hard disk.

The operating parameters of this folder can be found by choosing the command *Tools/Internet Options* (*General* tab). Click on the *Settings* button to display the options window.

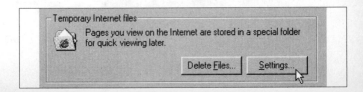

How cache operates

The first four options define the operating mode of Internet Explorer when you view a previously visited page (whose components are therefore present in the temporary Internet file).

Every visit to the page

If the page on the site has changed in comparison to what is in the cache, Internet Explorer downloads the new page and stores it in the temporary file.

Every time you start Internet Explorer

Internet Explorer also checks whether the page on the site is more recent than the one that is in the temporary file, but only if the page has not been consulted since you opened Internet Explorer. In other words, so long as you don't close Internet Explorer, when you visit the same page more than once it is only downloaded once. If the page has been modified on the site between two consultations in the same session, you would not see the modifications.

Automatically

As with the preceding option, Internet Explorer checks whether the contents of the page on the site are more recent than those stored in the cache file, only if the page has not been consulted since starting Internet Explorer. But, if Internet Explorer sees that the modifications on the site are not very frequent, the checks for that page will also be less frequent.

Never

Internet Explorer always displays the page present in the temporary folder without checking whether the page was modified on the site. So you will never see the modifications made to the pages on the site. This option saves time, but lacks efficiency.

The *Automatically* option is active by default.

By activating *Every time you start Internet Explorer*, you will see the latest version of each page displayed every time you start the program.

In order to be sure you are seeing the latest version of the page being displayed, download it again by clicking on the Refresh button or pressing *F5*.

Checking the cache

Still in the *Parameters* window, you can:

✓ see where the temporary folder is located;

✓ move it to another disk (if you have more than one hard disk, install it on the fastest one);

✓ modify its size (do not exceed 100 Mb).

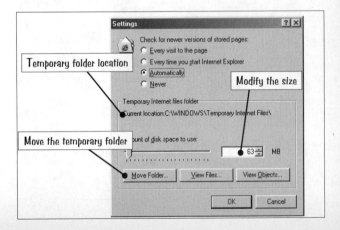

When the size indicated here has been reached, the oldest files are deleted to make room for the new ones.

By clicking on the *View File* button, you will open the temporary folder window and thus be able to view the files it contains.

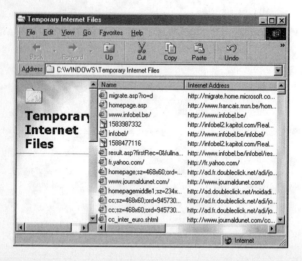

The window presents the files in a table with several columns. You can modify the width of the columns by dragging the right-hand border of their header. By clicking on a column header you can sort the table according to the contents of that column.

In this list, double-click on the address of a Web page to view it in the browser window. You can also view an image by clicking on its filename.

This temporary file is obviously a trifle indiscreet, since it keeps track of all your visits on the Web. You can empty it completely by clicking on the *Delete Files* button in the general dialogue box of Parameters.

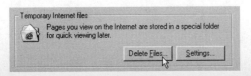

Keeping track of your surfing

The address of every Web page you visit is kept in memory, independently of the cache. This is the history of your visits. The folder of temporary Internet files stores the files themselves, while the *History list* only keeps the Web page addresses and classifies them by the dates when they were visited.

To open the history bar, click on the *History* button in the toolbar.

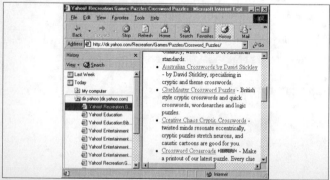

The Internet Explorer window is divided into two sections, on the left is the History bar and on the right is the navigation section.

You can modify the width of the sections by dragging the vertical separation bar with the mouse left or right.

To close the *History* bar, click on the little x at the top right-hand corner of the bar or click once more on the *History* button.

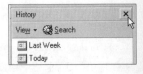

Viewing a page in History

The sites you have visited are organised chronologically. Today's sites are in the Today folder, whilst those from previous days and weeks are grouped together in other folders.

Each site is also represented by a folder containing the list of pages in the site that you visited.

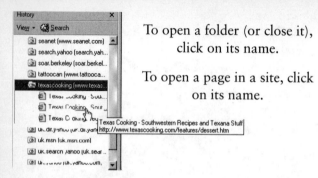

To open a folder (or close it), click on its name.

To open a page in a site, click on its name.

You'll see that if you position the mouse pointer over the name of a page, an info-bubble appears displaying its exact address.

Organising the History bar

The History bar is classified chronologically, but you can choose to use another method of classification.

Click on the *View* button in the *History* bar and select one of the methods offered:

- ✓ **By Date:** grouping by weeks (this is the default display mode).

- ✓ **By Site:** the sites are classified by name in alphabetical order.

- ✓ **By Most visited:** the pages are displayed by frequency of visit, starting with those you have consulted most often.

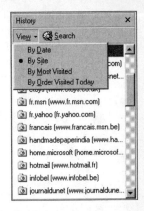

- ✓ **By Order visited today:** only the sites visited today are displayed, in chronological order.

Searching in the History bar

To find a site you visited recently, but of which you can't remember the exact name or address, conduct a search in the *History bar*.

Click on the Search button in the History bar.

 Type a word and click on the Search Now button.

Internet Explorer will delve through *History* to give you a list of pages containing this word, either in their title or in their address.

The period covered by History

By default, History keeps track of your visits for twenty days. If you want to modify this period, choose the command *Tools/Internet Options* and click on the *General* tab.

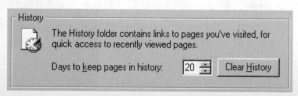

Type in the number of days that the History is to cover, which can be no more than 999.

If you don't want another user of your computer to be able to see the details of your visits on the Web, delete them by clicking on the *Clear History* button. History also provides the addresses of the sites you visited in the scroll-down list in the address zone of your browser. By deleting History, this list will be cleared as well.

Surfing offline

 This is a very useful feature if you have the type of agreement with your telecom operator where you pay for the time that you are connected to the Internet.

When you disconnect from the Internet, you can return to the pages that you visited by using the *Back* and *Forward* buttons (see pages 68). The pages remain stored in RAM so long as Internet Explorer remains open. But as soon as you close your browser, they will disappear.

However, the temporary file folder saves the pages you visit on the hard disk, so they remain available, even after closing your browser. This means that you can view them again without having to connect up to the Internet.

Open Internet Explorer and choose the command *File/Work Offline*. Then proceed as though your were still connected. You can enter the addresses of sites, click on links and surf from page to page without being online. You can also use History by clicking on the pages you want to view. Internet Explorer displays Web pages in the same format in which they were saved in the cache memory (the Temporary folder) when you first visited them.

If you position the cursor over a hypertext link associated with a Web page which is not in the cache, the little hand of your mouse pointer is accompanied by the 'forbidden' sign.

If you click on a 'forbidden' hypertext link or if you type in the address of a Web page that is not present in the cache, Internet Explorer will be unsure as to whether you want to stay offline or go online. However, in this instance you will have to go online to view the page.

4

Making use of data

Making use of data

After you have accessed and viewed the pages you can do the following:

- ✔ save Web pages;
- ✔ print them;
- ✔ copy text and images into the Clipboard;
- ✔ save an image.

Note

Make sure you stay within the law — do not distribute texts or images without the agreement of their owners. The Web is free, but that does not mean that you can plagiarise, copy and make use of data published on it without restriction.

Saving Web pages

If you have you discovered a Web page whose contents are of particular interest , you can save the whole thing, text and images, on to your hard disk. Choose the command *File/Save As*.
Open the folder in which you want to save the page. Give it another name if you wish. Finally, click on the *OK* button.

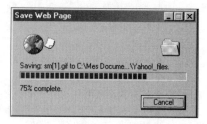

Once you have saved it, you will find the following on the hard disk, in the selected folder:

> A file with the suffix htm or html: it contains the text of the page and a link for each image displayed;

> A folder containing the images displayed in the page. The name of this folder is the same as the page, followed by the text '_files'.

For example, if you save a Web page under the name 'show', you will find the following on the hard disk:

> ✔ the file show.htm;
>
> ✔ the folder show_files.

show_files show.htm

If you move or copy the page's file, don't forget to move and copy the folder with which it is associated as well.

 Do not rename this folder: the Web page would then no longer be able to retrieve the pictures because it points to the picture file in the folder created when saving. For example, the page entitled show.htm is linked to pictures in the file called show_files.

Sending a Web page by mail

If you want to send a Web page by e-mail, you can choose between:

> sending the complete page in the message (not as an attachment file), your correspondent will see the page in his e-mail software;

sending the address of the page (your correspondent will have to click on the address to view the page in his or her browser).

Choose the command *File/Link by Email* or *File/Page by Email*.

Printing a Web page

The page setup

Before printing, check whether the page layout is suitable for you. Select the command *File/Page Setup*.

Choose the orientation of the paper.

Set the size of the margins, making sure that they are at least 10 mm (3/8 inch) wide.

Fill in the headers and footers. You can type in any text you want, as well as codes that will print automatic data.

&w   The title of the window.

&u   The address of the page.

&d   The date of printing in abbreviated form (see the module Regional Parameters in the Configuration Panel).

&D   The date of printing in full (see the module Regional Parameters in the Configuration Panel).

&t   The time of printing in the format defined in the module Regional Parameters in the Configuration Panel.

&T	The time in 24-hour format.
&p	The number of the printed page.
&P	The total number of pages.
&&	Printing the character &.
&btext	Centering the text
&btext1&btext2	Centering text1 and right justification of text2.

For example :

&bInternet&b&d - page &p will print:

> Internet   15/02/2000 - page 3

Printing

To print the page being displayed, choose the command *File/Print*.

Note that the print button does not open the dialogue box, but will print a copy of the Web page as you see it on the screen.

Copies

Indicate the number of copies to be printed.

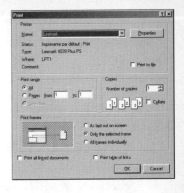

If you print several copies and you confirm the option Collate, the pages will be printed in the order in which they are assembled.

For example, the Web page you are printing requires three pages numbered 1, 2 and 3. You want two copies.

With the Collate option, the pages will be printed in the following order:

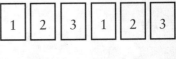

Without the Collate option, they will be printed like this:

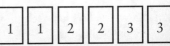

Frames

Some Web pages are made up of several frames. You can tell if this is the case by scrolling up or down the page. If part of the page doesn't move, it is in a different frame. Frames enable a Web page to contain several different elements at the same time without interfering with one another. You can print out the contents of each frame separately if you wish.

If you want to print the Web page as you see it on the screen, confirm the option *As laid out on screen*.

If you want to print just one of the frames, click on the relevant frame before choosing the command *File/Print* and confirm the option *Only the selected frame*.

For example: here is a Web page composed of three frames:

And finally, if you want to print each frame individually, confirm the option *All frames individually*.

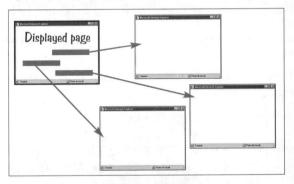

Linked pages

The option *Print table of links* is very useful, because it prints not only the current page, but also the list of hypertext links it contains. They are organised in two columns, the name of the link on one side and the address of the linked page on the other.

The option *Print all linked documents* is also useful as it will print not only the page being displayed, but also all the pages connected to it by a hypertext link.

If you want to print just one of the linked pages, don't open the print dialogue box, but click on the hypertext link of the page to be printed. Choose the command *Print Target* from the menu.

Clipboard

Instead of saving a complete page, you can copy a piece of text selected in advance and then paste it into another document (Word or Notepad, for example).

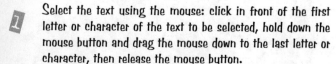

1   Select the text using the mouse: click in front of the first letter or character of the text to be selected, hold down the mouse button and drag the mouse down to the last letter or character, then release the mouse button.

2   Then choose the command Edit/Copy.

3   Activate the document in which you wish to insert the text currently contained in the Clipboard.

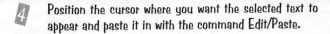

4 Position the cursor where you want the selected text to appear and paste it in with the command Edit/Paste.

You can't select text and images at the same time. If there are images in your selection, they will not be captured, but you can save and copy images individually (see below).

As the Web pages displayed in a browser are read-only, you cannot modify them, so the *Cut* command does not exist. It is therefore also impossible to delete anything from them, so the *Delete* command doesn't exist either.

The usual Clipboard buttons are not present in the toolbar, but the shortcut keys are just as effective:

[Ctrl]-[c]	Copy
[Ctrl]-[v]	Paste

You can also copy into the *Clipboard* the address to which a hypertext link refers. Click on the link with the right mouse button and choose the command *Copy Shortcut*. Then paste it into any other document you choose.

For example:

copy the link and, when you come to paste it into a document, you will be inserting the following text:

http://www. thecase. com

Images

As with text, images can be extracted from Web pages so you can save them on your hard disk.

Click on an image with the right mouse button and choose the appropriate command:

✓ *Save Picture As* to save it on your hard disk;

✓ *Set As Wallpaper* to turn it into wallpaper for your Windows Desktop;

✓ *Copy* to copy it into the Clipboard and then paste it into another document.

The image you choose as wallpaper will be displayed in the middle of your Desktop screen. If the image is small it will look rather lost on your screen, in which case you can enlarge it by stretching it, or multiply it into a mosaic to cover the whole of your Desktop screen.

Stretched image

Mosaic image

Click with the right mouse button anywhere on Windows Desktop and choose the command *Properties*. At the bottom of the dialogue box, open the *Display* list and select either *Stretch* or *Tile*.

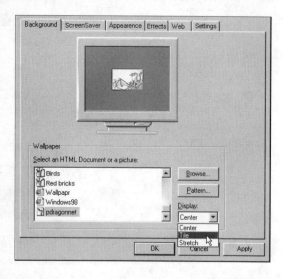

5

Favorites

Favorites

How do you save the addresses of the sites and pages you consider most important, so that you can revisit them easily and quickly? With Internet Explorer you save them in a special folder called *Favorites*.

You can organise the *Favorites* folder to suit your needs by inserting as many subfolders as you think necessary.

> ### Note
>
> When you save in Favorites you are not saving the addresses of whole sites, but rather the addresses of individual Web pages.

Saving a page in Favorites

When you see a page in the browser window whose address you want to save, insert it into the Favorites folder. Choose the command *Favorites/Add to Favorites*.

1 You'll see the title of the page, as chosen by the site's creator, in the Name box. You can save this name, or give it another one that you find more relevant or will mean more to you.

2 Then click on the OK button.

As you surf around the Web, your list of Favorites can get quite long making it difficult to locate the Web page you want quickly, which is, after all, the objective of the Favorites feature.

Favorites can be seen in the list that appears when you click on Favorites.

The way to solve this problem is to create subfolders in order to group together *Favorites* concerning a similar topic.

Subfolders

To save an address in a subfolder: choose the command *Favorites/Add to Favorites*.

 In the dialogue box, click on the button Create in.

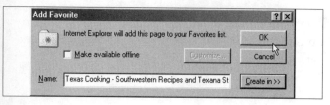

 Select the Favorites folder in which you wish to insert the address and click on OK. To create a new folder, click on the New Folder button.

 Type in the name of the folder you want to create and click on OK.

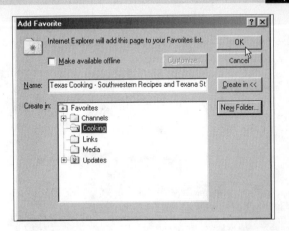

4 Finish by clicking on the OK button to insert the address into the new folder.

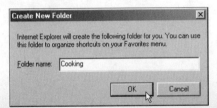

In this way you can create a system of subfolders. To create a new folder, just make sure you select the folder in which it is to be contained.

For example:

The folder *Mexican* will be created in the folder *Cooking*.

Creating a Favorite from a link

You don't have to view a page in order to record its address in *Favorites*. If you see a hypertext link to a page which interests you, click on it with the right mouse button and choose the command *Add to Favorites*. The address of the page connected to the link will then be inserted into *Favorites*.

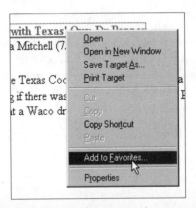

Using Favorites

If you collect Web page addresses in this way, it will make it easy for you to access them subsequently when you want to revisit a site.

To get to a page saved in Favorites:

1 Choose the command Favorites, which opens the list.

2 Position the cursor over the Folder (and if necessary, the various subfolders) in which the Favorite you're looking for is located. The folders open when you position the cursor over them for a moment (without clicking). This list operates in the same way as the Windows Start menu.

3 Click on the name of the Favorite you want to view.

4 Internet Explorer accesses the site and downloads the page exactly as though you had entered the address yourself in the address box.

The Favorites folder is also available in the *Start* menu, so you don't have to open Internet Explorer. As soon as you click on a *Favorite*, the browser automatically opens to begin downloading the page.

Managing Favorites

You can copy, delete, move, rename and classify Favorites and the folders they contain.

When you open the *Favorites* list, from the *Favorites* menu, click with the right mouse button on one of them and choose the appropriate command:

- ✓ Delete;
- ✓ Rename;
- ✓ Sort by name.

Organising Favorites

A single dialogue box enables you to organise your Favorites folder. To open this dialogue box, choose the command *Favorites/Organize Favorites*.

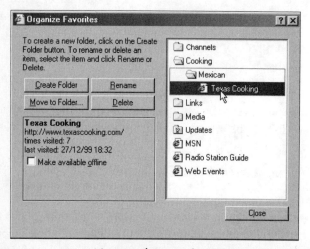

You open (and close) a folder
simply by clicking on its name.

When you select the name of a page, its address, the number of visits made to it and the date of your last visit will be displayed in the dialogue box.

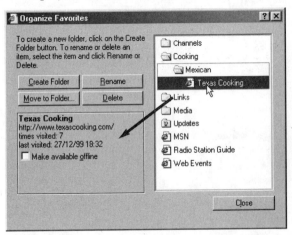

To create a new folder, select the subfolder in which it will be contained. Then click on the button *Create Folder*. The folder is inserted into the system.

It is called *New Folder* by default, so to rename it simply type in the name you want to give it.

For example:

the subfolder *Indian* is created in the folder *Cooking*.

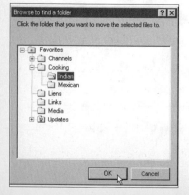

To delete or rename a folder or a Favorite, select it and click on the *Delete* or *Rename* button.

To move a folder or a Favorite into another folder, select it and click on the button *Move* to Folder. If you move a Favorite inside a folder, or in a folder which already contains Favorites, a black horizontal line will show where it will be moved to. Release the mouse button.

You can also move and reposition a folder using the mouse. Select the folder you want with the mouse and, holding the mouse button down, move the folder to its new position by dragging it with the mouse. If you move the *Favorite* inside the same folder or into a folder already containing *Favorites*, a black horizontal bar indicates its future location before you release the mouse button.

If you move it to another folder, release the mouse button when the destination folder has been selected.

Note that, as usual, you only need to position the cursor over a folder for a moment to open it.

If you want to cancel moving a folder, a file or a Favorite after you've started it, press *Esc*.

The Favorites list

By displaying *Favorites* in their own window, you can keep them handy for speedy use. Click on the *Favorites* button.

To close this window, click on the little cross (top right) or just click on the *Favorites* button once more.

The buttons *Add* and *Organize* are the same as the commands *Favorites/Add to Favorites* and also *Favorites/Organize Favorites*.

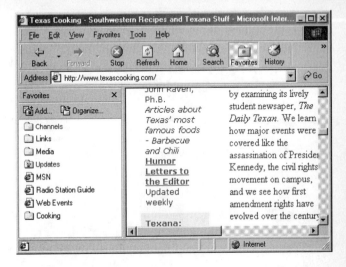

Once this window is open, inserting a new Favorite is very simple. When the page you wish to save is displayed, click on the little icon in the address box; hold down the mouse button and drag it into the *Favorites* list.

The black hori-
zontal bar indicates
its future location, so
then just position the
cursor over a folder
for a moment without
clicking to open it.

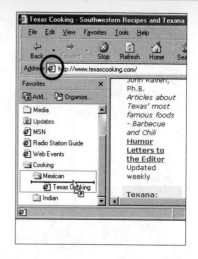

The *Esc* key allows you to cancel the current
operation if you make a mistake.

Again, you can move a folder or a Favorite just by
dragging it with the mouse.

You can rename or delete a folder or a Favorite by clicking on its name with the right-hand mouse button, the commands are in the drop-down menu.

Importing and exporting

Netscape Navigator saves favourite pages in a different way and calls them Bookmarks. They are saved in a file called *bookmark.htm* located in a *Users* subfolder.

To locate the *Bookmarks* file, carry out a search, click on the right-hand mouse button on *My Computer* and choose the command *Find*. In the *Name* box, type in bookmark and click on the *Find* button.

To export your favorites into a Bookmarks file

Choose the command File/Import and Export.

 Click on the Next button.

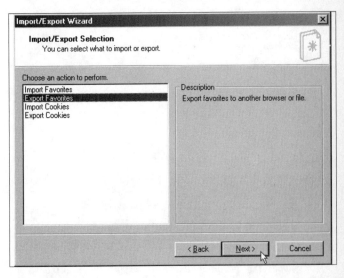

 Select **Export Favorites** and click on **Next**.

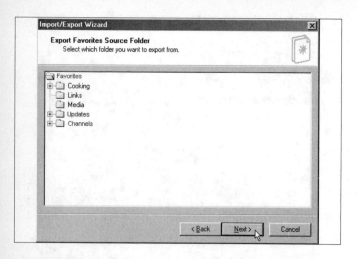

 Select the Favorites folder (to export them all) or a subfolder (to limit the export to this subfolder only). Click on Next.

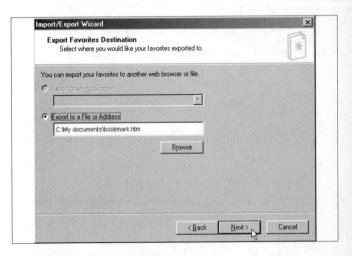

 Click on the Browse button to select the destination folder. If you wish, enter another name for the file. Don't forget that Netscape Navigator's bookmark file must be called bookmark.htm. Click on Next.

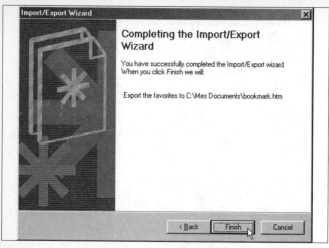

 Click on the Finish button. The export will now start.

You can also use this method for sending your Favorites to someone else (by email, for example): export them and attach the file you've created to your message.

To import a bookmark file

 Choose the same command File/Import and Export.

 Select Import Favorites.

 Select the bookmark file to be converted into Favorites.

 Then select the subfolder in Favorites where the bookmarks, once converted, will be inserted.

Saving a Favorite in your Desktop

Even though the Favorites folder is the best place to save pages to which you will often refer, you can also create a shortcut to a Web page in Windows Desktop. The term *Shortcut* is used rather than Favorite, even though you can use a Shortcut in exactly the same way as you do a Favorite.

 Display the Web page in the browser window for which you want to create a shortcut in Desktop.

2 If the browser window fills the whole screen, restore it by clicking the Restore button.

3 Drag the little icon in the address box on to your Desktop.

4 When you release the mouse button, the shortcut is created.

ALFRED
HITCHCOCK

With this same method you can create a shortcut in any folder.

For a quicker method

1 Click with the right mouse button in the Web page (make sure you don't click on any text or image).

2 Choose the command Create Shortcut.

3 A message tells you that the shortcut will be created. Click on OK.

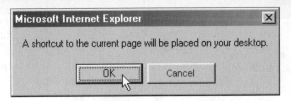

A double-click on the *Shortcut* icon will open the browser, which will then download the Web page.

The Startup page

When you open Internet Explorer, a default page is displayed automatically. If your browser is Explorer then the page is a Microsoft page, adapted to your country of residence. It is not part of Favorites and can be changed, so you can pick another Startup page if you prefer to do so.

 Display the Web page you want to use as the Startup page.

 Choose the command Tools/Internet Options (General tab).

Click on the button Use current.

The button *Use Default* will install the Microsoft page again, while the *Use Blank* button will open the browser window on a blank page.

6

Security

Security

There are various aspects to consider regarding security on the Web. First of all there is the **risk of viruses**. Though it is true that the Web is not the main carrier transmitting viruses, the risks are nevertheless real and you need to take a few precautions.

Checking cookies could be regarded as another security matter. A cookie is a piece of information that a Web site you have visited leaves on the hard disk of your computer, enabling it to recognise you the next time you visit it.

E-commerce raises the important question of how to **buy something online** using a credit card number. You need to be able to send information across the Net without any unauthorised computers being able to intercept it.

Finally, security is also a **parental concern** – the problem of how to allow your children to browse the Web, yet keep them protected them from sites whose contents are violent or pornographic.

Protecting yourself from viruses

Even though viruses are not often found on Web pages, there nevertheless is some risk of acquiring one. A virus is the computer version of a nasty bout of flu. It is a malignant little program that hides in files and so can be passed to any computer downloading files. Some viruses don't do any harm, they just multiply and spread themselves around, but most are bad news and will cause chaos, deleting or corrupting files, or even crashing the computer. On the Internet viruses originate in programs such as *ActiveX controls*, *JavaScripts* and *Java applets* which enable designers to add extra features to Web pages.

Choose the command *Tools/Internet Options* and click on the *Security* tab.

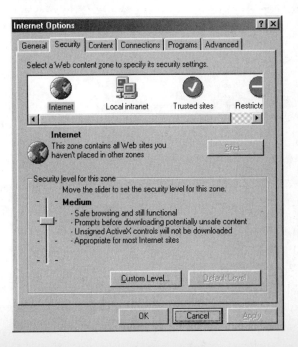

In this dialogue box you will see that Internet sites are set up to have a certain level of security. In practice, this means that a message will inform you that an application is included in a Web page before it downloads it to your computer and will first ask you to confirm your acceptance.

An antivirus program is indispensable as it will check all files downloaded to your computer to see if they contain any viruses. This check is carried out in different ways. One method bases the check on a list of more than 40,000 known viruses. The antivirus program knows the signatures of the viruses (a succession of codes clearly identifying a virus) and can check for the presence of these signatures in the files being downloaded. This list of signatures is constantly being updated to take account of new viruses. You must therefore download the updates regularly. The command for doing this is included in the antivirus software.

Here are three of the most efficient
antivirus programs :

✓ Norton Antivirus

✓ McAfee Antivirus

✓ AntiVirus Toolkit Pro

You will find a trial version of these antivirus
programs on the CDs that come with computer
magazines.

Cookies

Cookies are text files containing items of information transmitted to your computer by Web sites. They are saved on to your hard disk by your browser. When you return to a Web site that has deposited a cookie, the site can retrieve the cookie, read its contents and send you a new one in exchange. Cookies can only be retrieved and read by the site which transmitted them. In this way sites can keep track of your visits and obtain valuable marketing information about your habits.

 Some other 'cookie facts': a cookie cannot contain a virus; you can consult, copy and delete a cookie; your computer can store a maximum of 300 of them, without exceeding 20 on the same server.

So, what do they contain? The answer is, whatever the designer of the site wants to be recorded in them. For example, they can report back to the Web site on the type of computer and operating system you use (Windows 98 for example), the number of times you have visited the site, and the date of your last visit. If you make purchases on a site, the reference codes of the articles you are ordering are also stored in cookies. If you use a customisable site (such as MSN : *http://msn.co.uk*), the custom settings are stored in cookies.

So, where can you find the cookies? They will be in the Temporary Files Internet folder. To open this folder, choose the command *Tools/Internet Options* and click on the *Settings* button.

Then click on the *View Files* button. They are easy to pick out since they start with 'Cookie'. The addresses of the sites responsible for the cookies are highlighted.

The date each cookie was created is shown in the column headed *Last Modified* and the date when it was last updated in the column headed *Last Accessed*.

You can delete any cookie you like, just by pressing **Delete**.

Checking cookies

If you prefer to check the writing of each cookie at the time when the sites generate them, you should modify the security settings in Internet Explorer.

 Choose the command Tools/Internet Options and click on the Security tab.

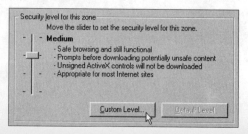

Click on the Custom Level button.

 Search for the category entitled Cookies.

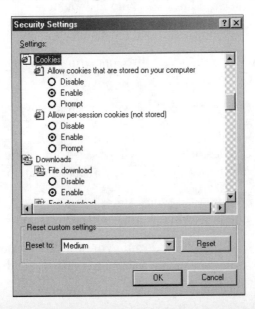

You will see that there are two types of cookies:

✓ Those that are deleted automatically every time you close Internet Explorer (not stored).

✓ Those that are saved permanently.

You have a choice of three operating options for each type of cookie:

Disable: no cookie will be saved on your hard disk;

Enable: the cookies will be saved automatically on your hard disk, without you being aware of it.

Prompt: each time a site is about to save a cookie, a message will ask for your confirmation.

If you choose the *Prompt* option, a message will inform you every time a site attempts to send you a cookie.

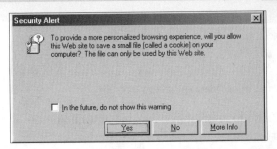

Click on the Yes button to accept the creation of a cookie.
Click on No to refuse it.

Once you have finished customising the security options, click on *OK*. A message will ask you to confirm the modifications you have made.

Secured pages

Some pages, especially those in shopping sites, are secured. These often contain a form to be completed with various items of personal information and, notably, a credit card number. The data on this form is sent back to the site when you click on the *Confirm* or *Submit* button provided by the site's designers. If this page is secured, the data will be encrypted before being sent and decrypted when it arrives, but it will not circulate unscrambled over the Net.

How do you know if a page is secured? Look at the far right of the status bar in Internet Explorer, a little

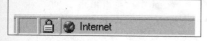

padlock indicates that the page on display is secured.

By double-clicking on this padlock, you will be able
to check the validity of the page's security.

Internet Explorer may display three messages relating to the security of pages.

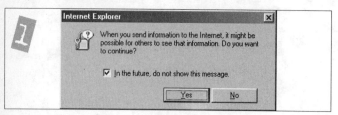

You have filled in a form on an unsecured page. The information you are about to send back to the site will not be encrypted. It will be passed unscrambled over the Net.

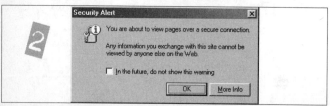

The page about to be displayed is secured.

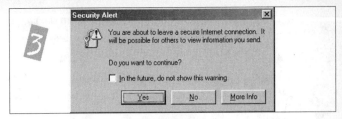

You are leaving a secured page.

The page about to be displayed is not secured.

Protecting children

If you have children whom you wish to protect from sites containing violence, sex, or obscenity use the Content Advisor to limit access to these sites.

 Select the Tools/Internet Options command.

 Click on the Content tab.

 Click on the Enable button.

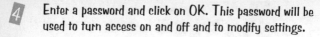

4 Enter a password and click on OK. This password will be used to turn access on and off and to modify settings.

5 Click on the Settings button.

6 Select the category: language, nudity, sex or violence.

7 Move the cursor to the desired level.

8 Click on OK to close the dialog box.

Access will be denied to sites which do not correspond to the level of protection you have selected.

Appendices

Appendices

Some addresses to get you started

Here is a short selection of sites that will enable you to take your first steps on the Web. As time goes by, you will no doubt add to this collection considerably. Don't forget to save in Favorites the ones you particularly like, or those to which you think you will often return.

Leisure and culture

The Louvre Museum

http://www.louvre.fr/louvrea.htm

From the Mona Lisa to Tutankhamun, a virtual visit to one of the finest museums in the world – without queuing or aching feet!

The Encyclopaedia Mythica

http://www.pantheon.org/mythica

One of the most extensive encyclopaedias devoted exclusively to mythology.

Montezuma, Oedipus, Amenhotep, Buddha: let us not forget all those who went before us so gloriously.

Tate Gallery

http://www.tate.org.uk

Visit the three galleries: London, Liverpool and St Ives: several collections can be viewed online.

Tate Gallery

Tintin

http://www. tintin. be

The famous Belgian reporter is always on the front page. The books, the characters, the insults of Captain Haddock, themed files (on the Unicorn, the Stratocruiser H-22, etc.). A whole world of its own – not forgetting Snowy of course.

NME

http://www. nme. com

The Web version of the famous New Musical Express. Daily events, reviews, extracts, concert dates.

The Internet Movie Database

http://www. imdb. com

An impressive database that aims to list all the information available on films. Search by title, actor's name, or character.

Art Crimes: The Writing on the Wall

http://www. graffiti. org

A gallery of graffiti art from cities all over the world. The first graffiti site on the Net. Helps preserve and document this transient art.

ChannelSeek

http://w2. channelseek. com

Hundreds of radio and TV channels are broadcast on the Net. They are all listed here. Today you can surf to the sound of samba and tomorrow to the rhythm of 1950s jazz.

Lonely Planet

http://www.lonelyplanet.com

Want to get away from it all, to distant horizons and exotic lands? Obtain folders, pictures and reports before you set off.

The quest for knowledge

Encarta

http://encarta.msn.com

16,000 articles for this encyclopaedia coupled with a complete atlas of the world. Published by Microsoft.

ENCARTA®

Atlapedia

http://www.atlapedia.com

A geographical and political map of all the countries in the world. Includes information about climate, demography, history and religion.

3D Atlas Online

http://www.3datlas.com

A superb atlas. For every country: a brief history, a contour map, a photo and addresses of sites.

Space.com

http://www.space.com

The great space adventure, the discovery of the solar system, the exploration of Mars. Superb images and clear explanations to help you find out everything about the universe.

Britannica

http://www.britannica.com

The Encyclopaedia Britannica in full, plus a selection of sites and books relating to the articles.

Sports

CricInfo

http://www-uk.cricket.org

The latest cricketing information throughout the world, national and international tours, numerous photos, statistics and personal files on the players.

UK Soccer

http://www.uk-soccer.com

Football in the UK and Europe for the football crazy. Match and championship results, statistics and commentaries.

Planet Rugby

http://www.planet-rugby.com

Everything to do with this robust contact sport. Matches in the UK and throughout the world, screensavers in the colours of famous teams, records, etc.

Daily life

iVillage

http://www.ivillage.com

A Web site for women of all ages; covering every aspect of a woman's life. 'How to get the most out of life and how to help each other do it.'

The Met. Office

http://www.meto.govt.uk

What will it be today? Umbrella or baseball cap? Grandma's hand-knitted sweater or T-shirt? Weather forecasts will enable you to make up your mind.

EuroTV

http://www.eurotv.com

The schedule of all TV channels, including satellite.

The National Lottery

http://www.national-lottery.co.uk

The official site of the British National Lottery. You can find information on the latest draws and learn how the money is used each time 'it couldn't be you'.

KidsHealth

http://kidshealth.org

Sore tummies, or serious infections, nutrition, growth and behaviour – parents as well as children can find explanations for their worries.

Family Tree Maker

http://www.familytreemaker.com

470 million names and more than 40,000 sites linked to their genealogies. Find out if you have any black sheep to hide, or family jewels to claim.

Yell

http://wwweyp.co.uk

Yellow Pages on the Net, also offering up-to-the minute information, e.g. weather forecasts for different holiday destinations around the world.

Shopping

Amazon

http://www.amazon.co.uk

Choose books, CDs, and videos from a huge catalogue. Pay with your credit card and your order will be delivered a few days later.

British Shopping

http://www.british-shopping.com

You can buy anything on the Internet. You don't believe it? Then you haven't seen this index yet! The selection is so vast you won't know where to start.

FS Auctions

http://www.fsauctions.co.uk

Auction sales on the Internet? You see the opening price, the top offer, the date and finish time of the auctions; join in by e-mail if you want to make a bid.

Reserved for children

Disney

http://disney.go.com

The enchanted world of Walt Disney, Disneyland, the Disney Channel, the Disney shop – as well as games, stories, treasures, villains and animal of the month.

Kids Domain

http://www.kidsdomain.com

Impossible to get bored here. If you don't want to cook, play games, or make presents, you can always go surfing on the numerous other sites on offer.

Gus Town

http://www.gustown.com

Everything's here in this little town, a post office for sending a postcard, your friends, a museum for making works of art, the library where you can read a great story and the restaurant.

Humour

JokesPlus

http://www.jokesplus.freeserve.co.uk

Have you heard the one about - religion, golf, the office, school, doctors, lawyers, etc?

Late Show

http://marketing.cbs.com/tvshows/mini/lateshow

David Letterman, direct from New York, top video excerpts, when the next broadcast is scheduled – just about everything to do with the famous talk show and its host.

A bit further afield..

Yahoo!

http://uk.yahoo.com

One of the most frequently consulted directories on the Internet. The sites are classified by category with the facility of searching by keywords.

Northern Light

http://www.northernlight.com

A fast, detailed and accurate directory. Also features financial information and a special business section.

Alta Vista

http://www.altavista.com

Search the World Wide Web in 25 languages, one of the best of the search engines.

altavista: SEARCH

Alexa.com

http://alexa.com

Adds the information people don't include on their Web sites, e.g. where they are located geographically, how many visits the site receives, etc.

Ask Jeeves

http://www.askjeeves.com

A powerful and reliable search engine.

PC shortcut keys

Here are the shortcut keys you can use with Internet Explorer.

The window

❏ To view Help on Internet Explorer or, in the dialogue box, to view Help in relation to a particular item: [F1]

❏ To switch between *Full screen* and *Normal* modes in the browser window: [F11]

❏ To open a new window: [Ctrl][n]

❏ To close the active window again: [Ctrl][w]

❏ To open a search in the exploration box: [Ctrl][e]

❏ To open Favorites in the exploration box: [Ctrl][i]

❏ To open History in the exploration box: [Ctrl][h]

❏ To open several folders in History or Favorites: [Ctrl] click

Surfing

❏ To go to the start page: [Alt][Home] [Ctrl] [h]

❏ To go to the next page: [Alt][right cursor]

❏ To go to the preceding page: [Alt][left cursor]

❏ To stop downloading a page: [Esc]

❏ To go to a new position:

[Ctrl][o]
or
[Ctrl][l]

❏ To activate a selected link:

[Enter]

Consulting a Web page

❏ To move forwards between the elements of a Web page, the address box and the links bar:

[Tab]

❏ To move backwards between the elements of a Web page, the address box and the links bar:

[Shift][Tab]

❏ To view the drop-down menu of a link:

[Shift][F10]

❏ To advance through frames: [Ctrl][Tab] or [F6]

❏ To scroll back to the beginning of a document: [up arrow]

❏ To scroll down to the end of a document: [down arrow]

❏ To scroll back, in larger intervals, to the beginning of a document: [Page up]

❏ To scroll down, in larger intervals, to the end of a document: [Page down] or [Spacebar]

❏ To go to the beginning of a document: [Home]

❏ To go to the end of a document: [End]

❏ To search in a page: [Ctrl][f]

❏ To update the active Web page only if the date of the Web version and that of the version on display are different: [F5] or [Ctrl][r]

❏ To update the active Web page even if the date of the Web version and that of the version on display are identical: [Ctrl][F5]

❏ To save the current page: [Ctrl][s]

❏ To print the current page or the active frame: [Ctrl][p]

❏ To copy the elements selected to Clipboard: [Ctrl][c]

❏ To select all the elements on the active Web page: [Ctrl][a]

The address box

❏ To select the text from the address bar: [Alt][d]

❏ To view History from the address bar: [F4]

❏ In the address bar, to place the cursor left of the preceding back slash (the character /): [Ctrl][left cursor]

❏ In the address bar, to place the cursor right of the following back slash (the character /): [Ctrl][right cursor]

❏ To add 'www.' At the beginning and '.com' at the end of the text typed into the address bar: [Ctrl] [Enter]

❏ To move forwards in the list of addresses entered semi-automatically: [↑]

❏ To move backwards in the list of addresses entered semi-automatically: [↓]

Managing Favorites

❏ To add the current page to your Favorites:

[Ctrl][d]

❏ To open the dialogue box Organize Favorites:

[Ctrl][b]

❏ To move the selected element upwards in the Favorites list in the dialogue box Organize Favorites:

[Alt] [↑]

❏ To move the selected element downwards in the Favorites list in the dialogue box Organize Favorites:

[Alt] [↓]

Mac shortcut keys

The shortcut keys below can be used with Internet Explorer.

The window

❑ Open a new window:

❑ Open the exploration box:

❑ Quit:

 N

 E

 Q

Surfing

❑ Return to previous page:

❑ Go to next page:

❑ Update subscriptions:

 (

)

 U

❏ Open a file on your hard disk: O

❏ Stop downloading a page: Esc

❏ Go to a new location: L

Consulting a Web page

❏ To scroll down a document quickly: [Page Down]

❏ To scroll up a document quickly: [Page Up]

❏ To go to the beginning of the page: [Home]

❏ To go to the end of the page: [End]

❏ To refresh the current page: R

❏ To display the source code
of a Web page:

 E

❏ To print the page:

 P

❏ To automatically fill in the common fields in a Web form (you must first have filled in the information form in automatic fill-in Profile located in the Edit menu):

 =)

Managing Favorites

❏ Add a Web site to your Favorites

 D

❏ Organize Favorites

 J

❏ Insert a Favorite manually

 K

The PC toolbar

Here are the toolbar buttons for Internet Explorer.

 Displays the previous page in the History of pages viewed. By clicking on the little arrow, the list of previous pages is displayed. Click on the one you want to view again.

 Displays the next page in the History of pages viewed. The little arrow opens the list of following pages.

 Stops downloading the current page.

 Downloads the page displayed once more.

 Displays the Web page chosen as the startup page in the dialogue box for Internet options.

Opens the search window to find sites using keywords.

 Opens the left-hand window in the contents of the Favorites folder.

 Opens the left-hand window in the History of pages visited previously.

 Opens the electronic mail application.

 Prints the page displayed.

 Opens the page displayed in Frontpage Express. By clicking on the arrow you will be able to choose another Web page editor installed in your system.

The Macintosh toolbar

Here are the buttons on the Internet Explorer toolbar:

 Displays the previous page in the History of pages viewed. By clicking on the little arrow, the list of subsequent pages is displayed. Click on the one you want to view.

 Displays the next page in the History of pages viewed. The little arrow opens the list of preceding pages.

 Stops downloading the current page.

 Downloads the page displayed once more.

 Displays the Web page chosen as the startup page in the dialogue box for Preferences.

 Opens the Favorites tab.

Opens the tab on the History of pages visited previously.

 Opens the search tab to find sites using keywords.

 Automatically fills in the areas on the form present on the page displayed.

 Increases the font size of the page displayed.

 Reduces the font size of the page displayed.

 Prints the page displayed.

 Opens the mailing software.

 Opens the Preferences dialogue box.

Glossary

Access provider: company that provides access to the Internet by subscription. See also Internet Service Provider.

ADSL: Asymmetric Digital Subscriber Line. ADSL enables computer data to be transferred at high speed over a standard telephone cable and therefore facilitates Internet connections about 30 times faster than by normal telephone call.

Animated GIF : image containing several consecutive GIF format images used to create animation. The animation can be viewed in an Internet browser.

Baud: the speed at which a device transmits data, measured by the variation or change in a communication channel, e.g. a telephone line. One baud can represent several bits.

Bit: contraction of binary digit. The bit is the smallest unit of information. The binary system is a counting system which computers use, consisting of just two digits (1 and 0).

Bits per second: indicate the flow-rate of data transfer. Bps are often used to define the connection speed of modems to the Internet. Be careful not to confuse Bits per second with bauds.

Bps: Bits per second.

Bookmarks: keep lists of your favourite Internet sites in the Netscape Navigator browser, enabling you to return to a site quickly and easily without having to look up and type in its address again.

Browser: program making it possible to view Web pages and their contents. The most popular are Internet Explorer and Netscape Navigator.

Byte: eight bits in any combination, e.g. 10010010. A computer's memory capacity is measured in bytes. A byte equals one character, e.g. 'book' is four bytes and so takes up four bytes in the the computer's memory storage.

Cable modem : makes it possible to connect up to the Internet through cable TV wiring, as long as the TV operator provides this service. As with ADSL, the connection is permanent.

Client: Computer accessing a server.

Connect: the action of joining the Internet. A modem is generally necessary to connect up.

Cookie: information copied into a file on your hard disk by a Web site when you visit that site, e.g. number of times you visited the site, pages visited, etc. The Web site can then retrieve that information when you revisit it.

Digitised: see ISDN.

Downloading: retrieving files or Web pages from another computer connected to the Internet and transferring them on to your computer.

Favorites: keep lists of your favourite Internet sites in the Internet Explorer browser. They enable you to return to a site you have previously visited quickly and easily without having to enter its address again.

File: a file contains computer data. It may contain any kind of information, e.g. text, images, a program. Files are given names and extensions. For example: cloud.jpg is a file containing an image. See also JPG.

Flash: program making it possible to create animation and interactive presentations that can be viewed in a Web page. They can be viewed with the aid of the plug-in Shockwave.

Gb: Gigabyte.

GIF: Graphic Interchange Format – compressed image format used to store images on a Web page. See also JPEG and Animated GIF.

Gigabyte: one gigabyte equals 1,073,741,824 bytes (more than a billion bytes).

HTML: HyperText Markup Language. HTML is the language used to create pages on the Internet. Among other things, HTML makes it possible to create hypertext links.

HTTP: HyperText Transfer Protocol forms the basis of Web technology. The set of rules governing the software that transfers HTML files and elements linked to them (images, animation, etc.) on the Internet. See also HTTP server.

HTTP server: a computer which puts sites (made up of HTML files) and the elements of which they are composed (images, Java applets, etc.) at the disposal of Internet users.

Hypertext: text containing links connecting you instantly to another place within the same Web page, to another page, or to another site. All the HTML pages in the Internet, as well as most of the Help files, make use of hypertext.

Interface: the portion of a program that interacts with the user.

Internet: world-wide network linking millions of computers together. The Internet makes it possible to access Web sites and e-mail, among other things.

Internet address: address assigned to a Web site, e.g. http://www.yahoo.com.

Internet Service Provider: company providing access to the Internet by subscription. See also Access Provider.

IP address: Interconnection Protocol address consisting of a series of four numbers (ranging from 0 to 255) assigned to every computer connected on the Internet for purposes of identification. For each IP address, there is an equivalent in words and letters, which is easier to memorise, e.g. 206.132.15.12 is the IP address of the Encyclopaedia Britannica and is the numerical equivalent of http://www.britannica.com.

ISDN: Integrated Services Digital Network. A digital network capable of transmitting computer data along telephone lines at high speed, a maximum of 128 Kb/sec. See also ADSL and Cable modem.

ISP: Internet Service Provider.

Java: programming language recognised by all the latest browsers, making it possible to insert animations, interactivity, sound, etc. into Web pages. See also Java Applet and JavaScript.

Java Applet: small program written in the Java programming language, that can be downloaded from a Web site. See also JavaScript

JavaScript: program in Java language written directly into an HTML page. Allows Web site designers to enhance the basic features provided by HTML. See also Java Applet.

JPEG: Joint Photographic Expert Group. Compressed image format used to store images on a Web page, often used for photographic images as opposed to simpler pictures with less colours. See also GIF.

JPG: See JPEG.

Kb/s: number of kilobytes travelling per second. This is a unit often used to define the download speed of a file.

Kilobyte (Kb): unit of measurement of storage space for data in the computer. One kilobyte equals 1,024 bytes (more than a thousand bytes).

Link: connects pages across the Web, takes you instantly to another page or Web site. See also Hypertext.

Login: name assigned to a user to access a server, e.g. to connect to the Internet.

Mb: Megabyte.

Megabyte: unit of measurement of storage space for data in the computer. One megabyte equals 1,048,576 bytes (more than a million bytes).

Modem: contraction of Modulator-Demodulator. A modem makes it possible to connect to the Internet via a traditional telephone line. When leaving the computer; the digital data is converted into analogue data (modulation), appropriate for travelling over the telephone network. When coming in to the receiving computer, the analogue data is converted back into digital data (demodulation) so that it can be processed by the computer.

Net: see Internet.

Netiquette: defines the ethics of the Net and the rules of good behaviour. You can see examples at the following address, http://www.dtcc.edu/cs/rfc1855.html.

Netscape Communicator: a series of free programs dedicated to using the Internet. Contains a browser and a program for managing e-mail.

Netscape Navigator: free browser software that is part of the Netscape Communicator suite produced by the Netscape company.

Network: a group of computers linked together. The Internet is a network.

Plug-in: small program added to a software program to give it extra functions, e.g. Shockwave is a plug-in for Internet browsers that enables Flash animations to be displayed.

Protocol: rules defining the manner in which data is transmitted between two computers, e.g. HTTP is the transfer protocol for Web page data.

Secured page: on the Web a secured page transmits information securely, e.g. a credit card number between your computer and a server. The protocol used most often is SSL.

Server: computer providing a specific service on any kind of network (including the Internet). The computer that accesses a server is called a client, e.g. an HTTP server.

Shockwave: plug-in that is necessary for displaying animations created with Flash.

Site: collection of Web pages containing text and multimedia elements, accessed through an address typed into a browser. For example: http://www.britannica.com is the Internet address of the Encyclopaedia Britannica's site.

SSL: abbreviation for Secure Socket Layer, the protocol most often used for secured connections on the Internet. See also Secured page.

Surfing: Using a browser to visit sites on the Internet.

Text file: file containing text without layout. i.e. no styling of letters (italics, bold) or presentation of the text (justification, indentation ,etc.).

URL: Abbreviation for Uniform Resource Locator. See Internet Address .

Web: See World Wide Web.

WebMaster: the person responsible for a site, usually the person who created it.

World Wide Web: all the Web pages of all the Internet sites grouped together.

WWW: World Wide Web.

Index